This is Badminton House.

Badminton is said to
have been invented here.

In badminton, a shuttlecock is hit
back and forth across a net.

You must attempt to keep the shuttlecock from hitting the ground.

A badminton court

The court is marked up for singles and doubles matches.

The net is 5 feet (or 1.5m) tall.

A badminton racket has a thin handle and strings across the head.

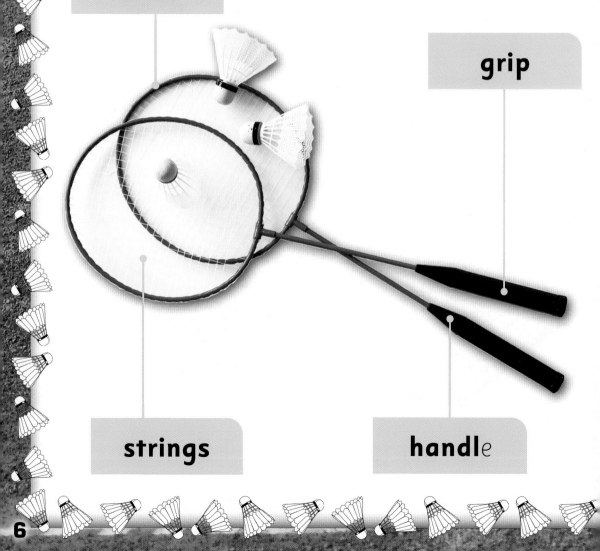

head

grip

strings

handle

Up until the 1900s, badminton rackets had "cat gut" strings. Cat gut comes from a cat's tummy!

Modern rackets have plastic strings.

To begin with, shuttlecocks had cork tops with sixteen feathers around them.

feather

plastic

Modern shuttlecocks are plastic.

The heavy cork top is
hit with the racket.

cork

Points are scored when the shuttlecock hits the ground in the court.

The scorer gets the next serve.

The serve must be hit up with an underarm swing. You must score 21 points to win the match.

serve

The shortest recorded badminton match was in 1996 in Hong Kong.

It was just
6 mins long!